FIRST TIME ALPHABET WORKBOOK

MICHEL MARCHESSEAULT

Trace and Color the Alphabet

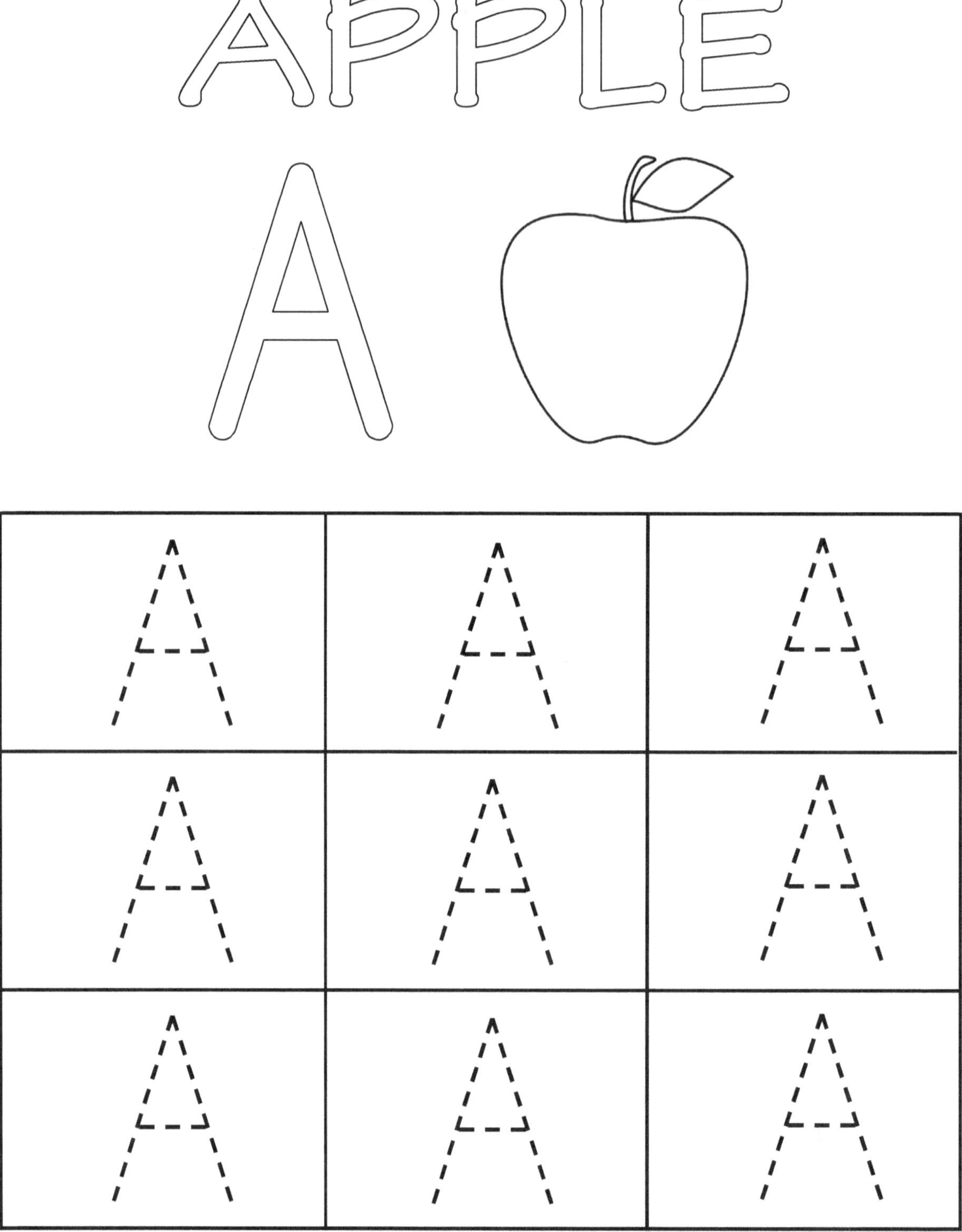

Trace and Color the Alphabet

BALL

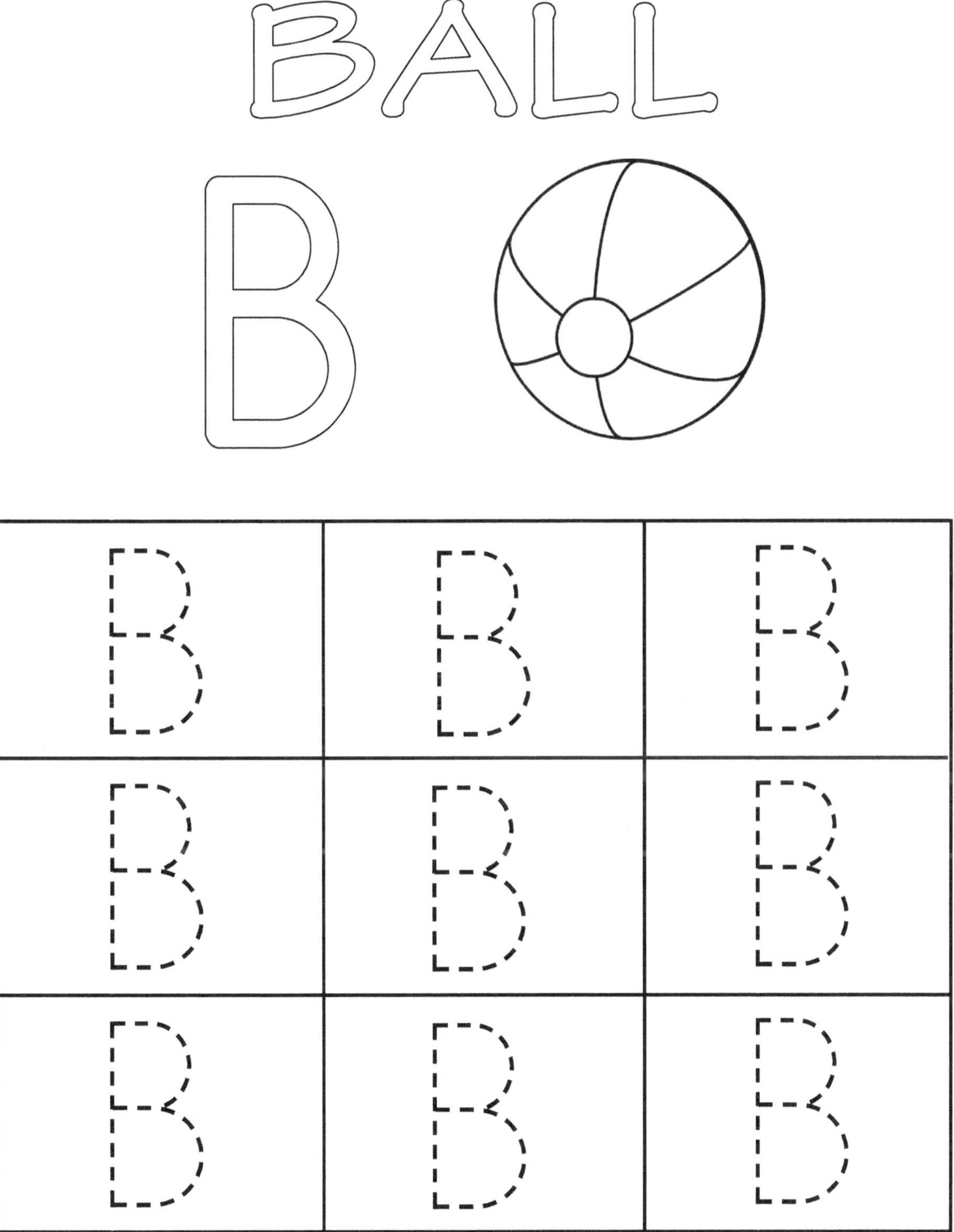

Trace and Color the Alphabet

Trace and Color the Alphabet

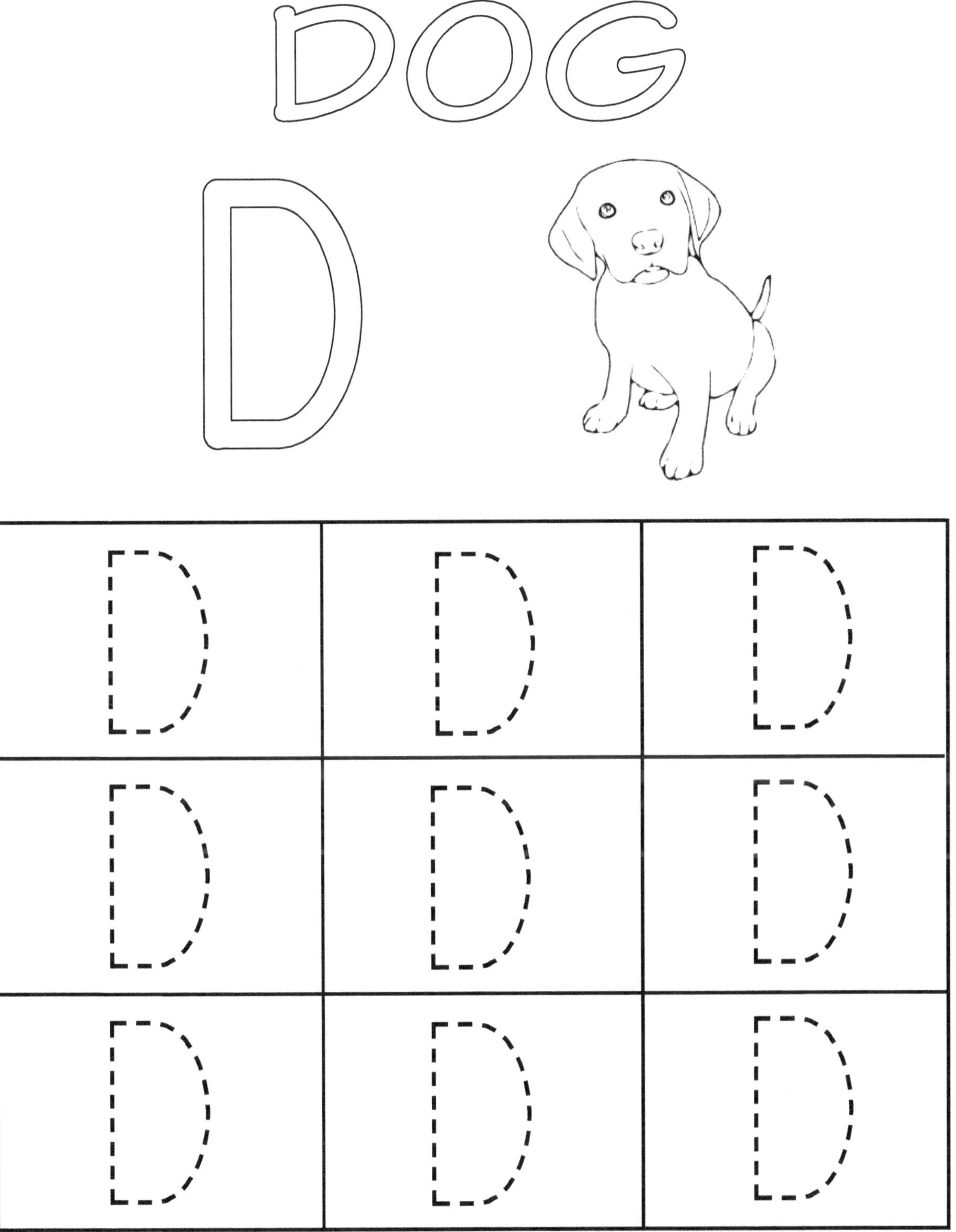

Trace and Color the Alphabet

ELEPHANT

Trace and Color the Alphabet

FISH

F

Trace and Color the Alphabet

Trace and Color the Alphabet

Trace and Color the Alphabet

INSECT

I

Trace and Color the Alphabet

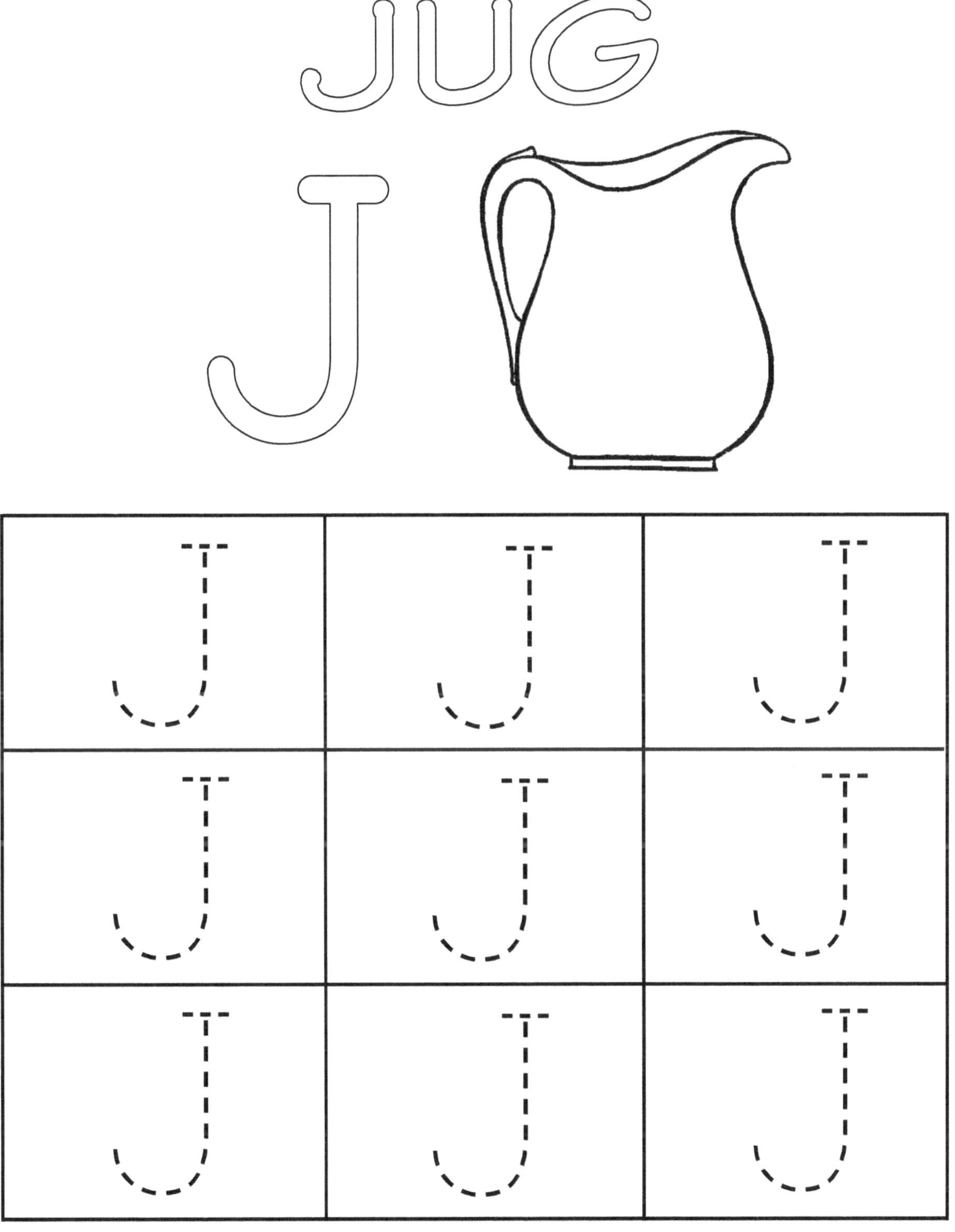

Trace and Color the Alphabet

Trace and Color the Alphabet

Trace and Color the Alphabet

MONKEY

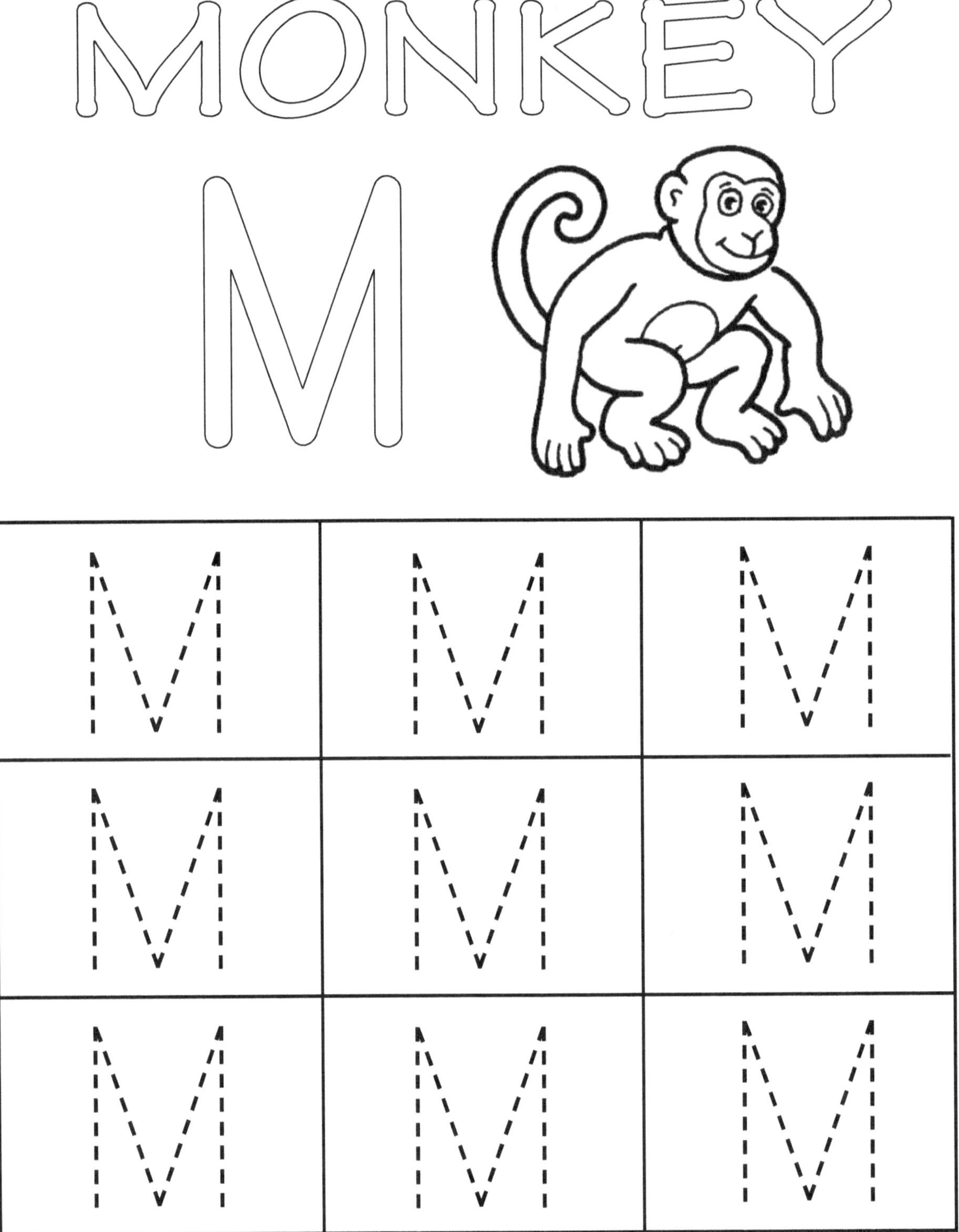

Trace and Color the Alphabet

NEST

N

Trace and Color the Alphabet

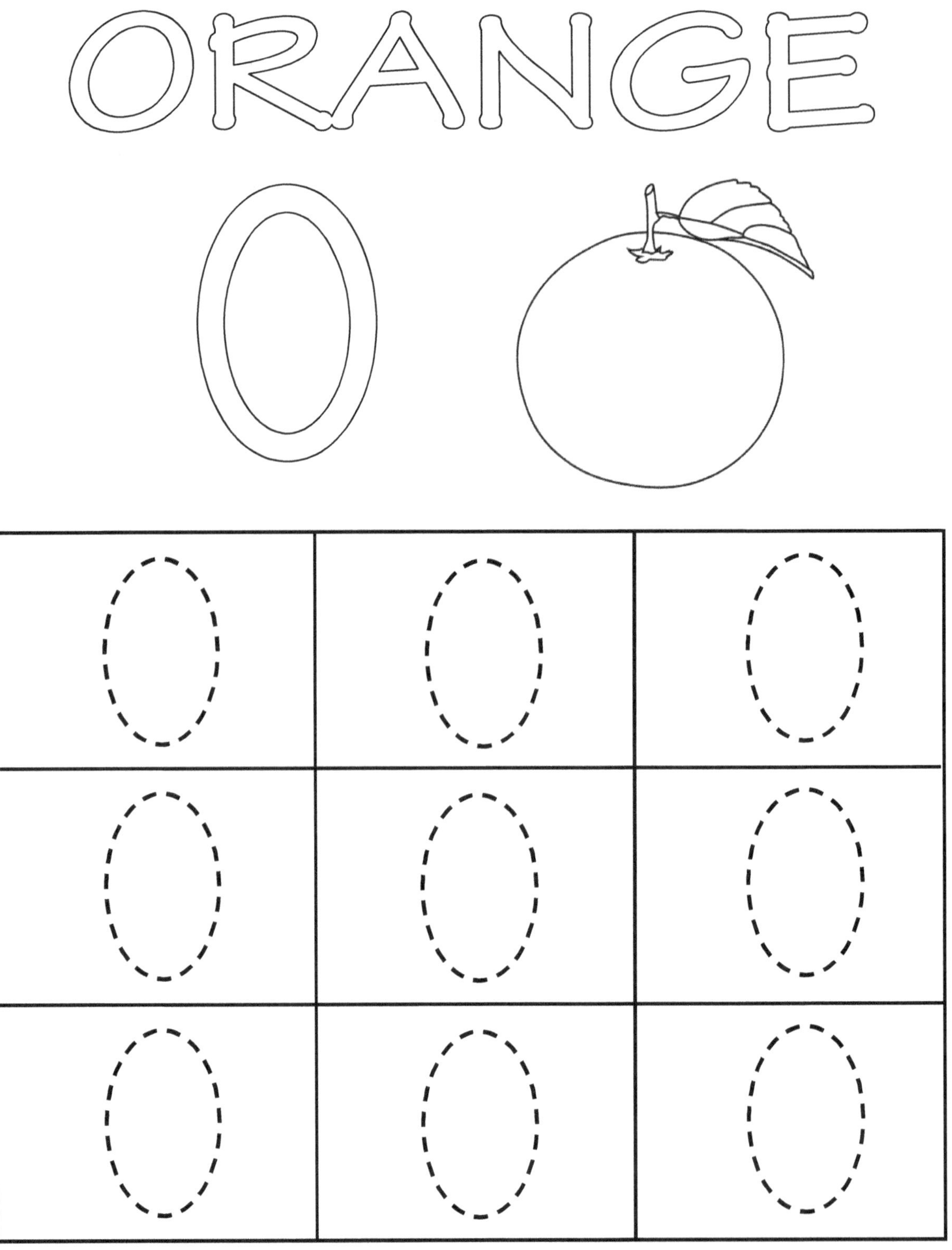

Trace and Color the Alphabet

Trace and Color the Alphabet

Trace and Color the Alphabet

Trace and Color the Alphabet

Trace and Color the Alphabet

TORTOISE
T

Trace and Color the Alphabet

UMBRELLA

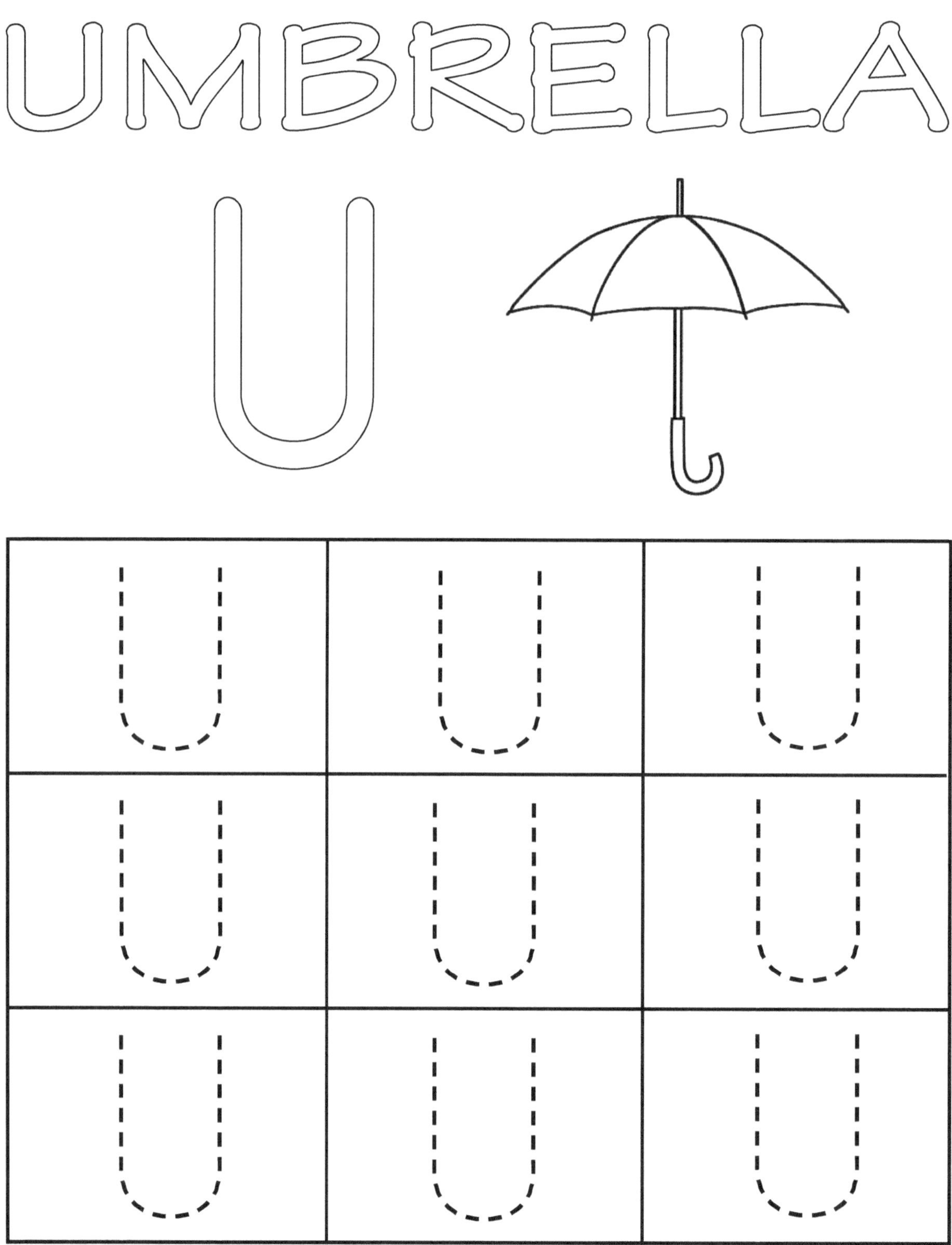

VULTURE

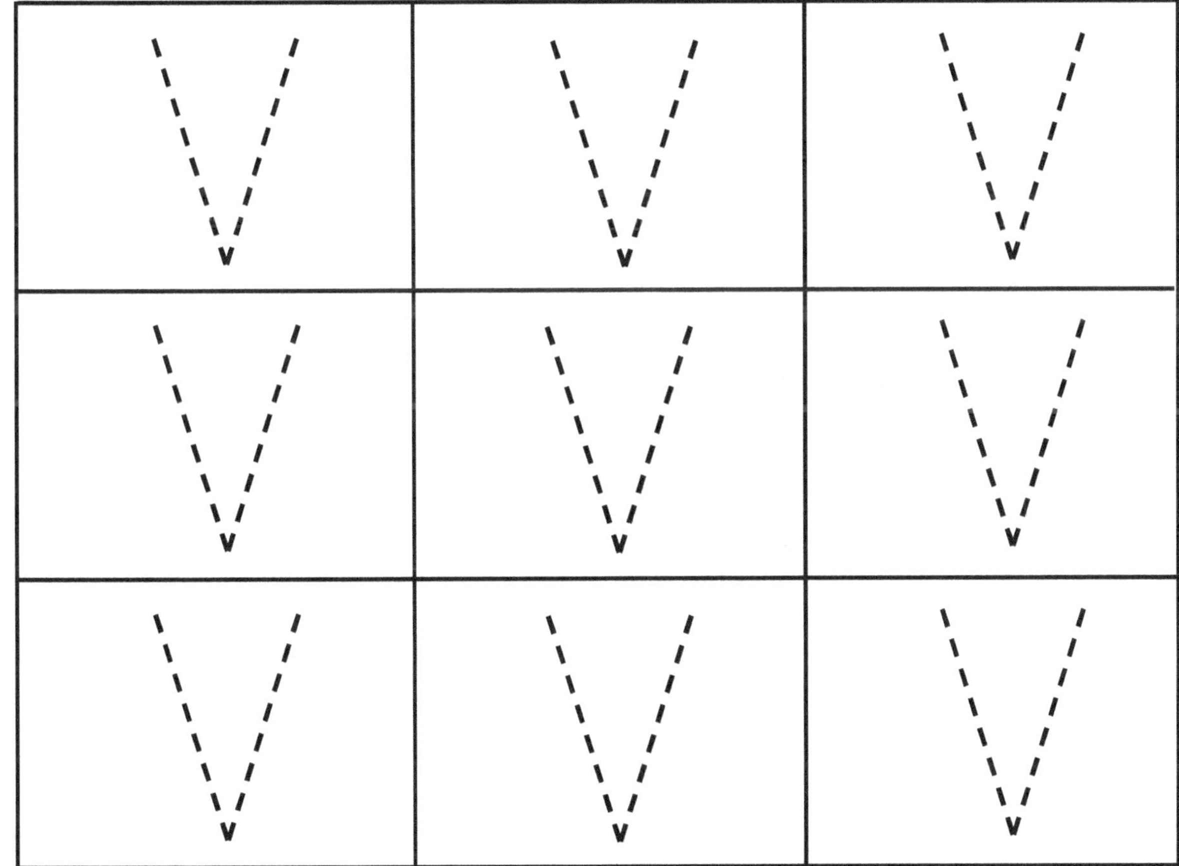

Trace and Color the Alphabet

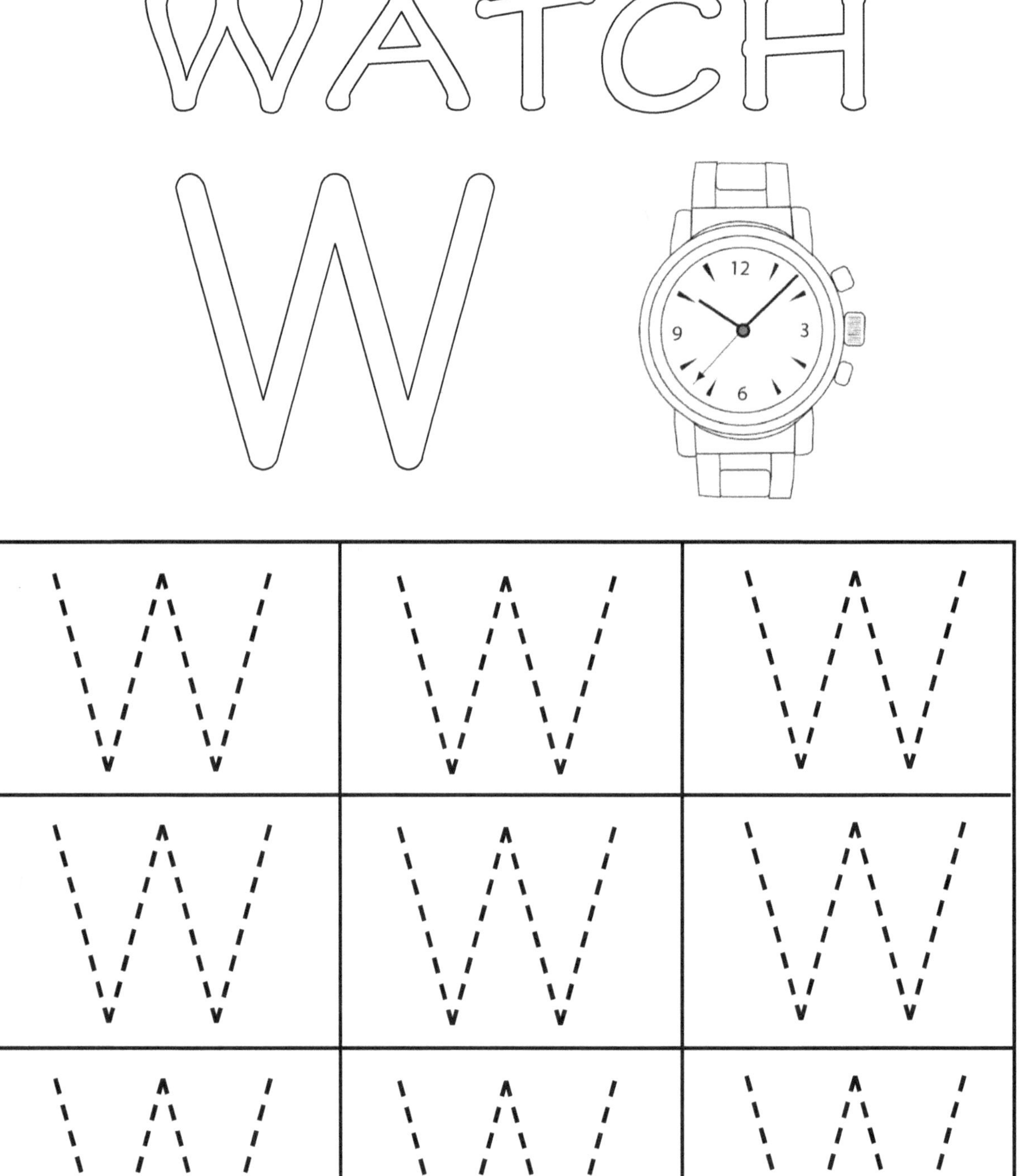

Trace and Color the Alphabet

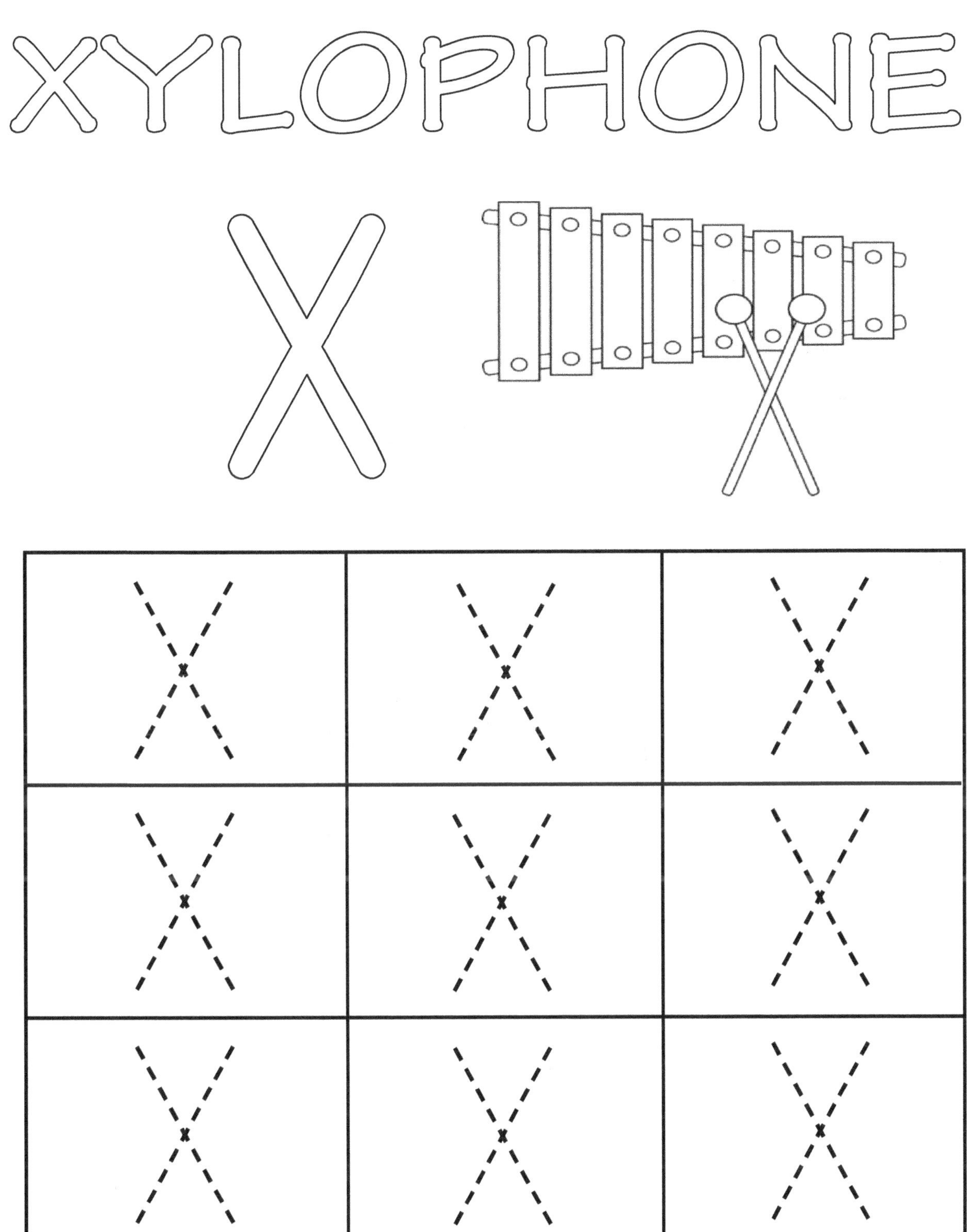

Trace and Color the Alphabet

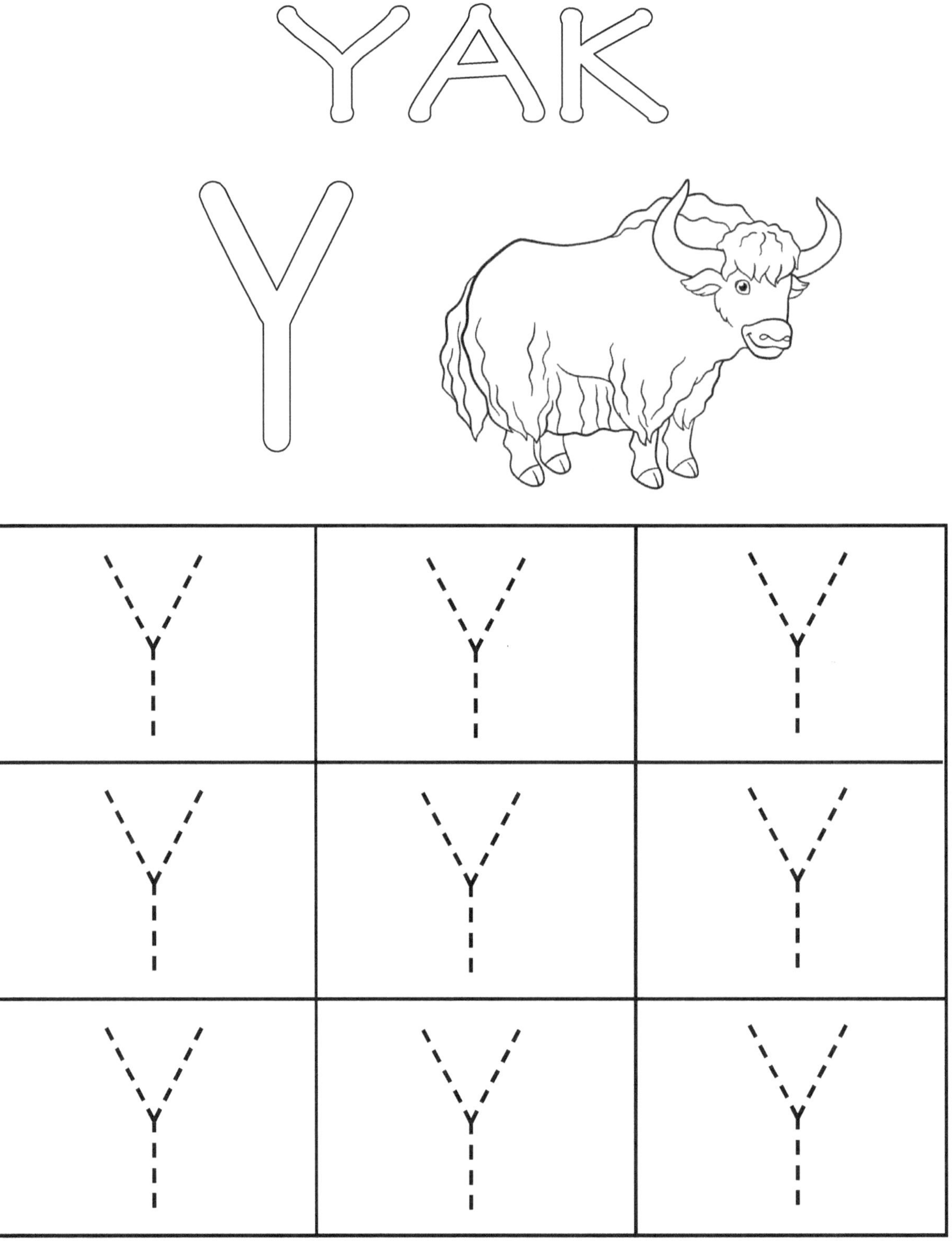

Trace and Color the Alphabet

ZEBRA

Z